A Guide for Using

Mr. Popper's Penguins

in the Classroom

Based on the novel written by Richard and Florence Atwater

This guide written by Rebecca Paigen

Teacher Created Materials, Inc.
6421 Industry Way
Westminster, CA 92683
www.teachercreated.com
©1997 Teacher Created Materials, Inc.
Reprinted, 2003
Made in U.S.A.
ISBN 1-55734-549-X

Edited by
Dona Herweck Rice

Illustrated by
Barb Lorseyedi

Cover Art by
Kelly McMahon

Table of Contents

Introduction

A good book can touch our lives like a good friend. Within its pages are words and characters that can inspire us to achieve our highest ideals. We can turn to it for companionship, recreation, comfort, and guidance. It can also give us a cherished story to hold in our hearts forever.

In Literature Units, great care has been taken to select books that are sure to become good friends!

Teachers who use this literature unit will find the following features to supplement their own valuable ideas.

- Sample Lesson Plan

- Pre-reading Activities

- Biographical Sketch and Picture of the Authors

- Book Summary

- Vocabulary Lists and Suggested Vocabulary Activities

- Chapters grouped for study, with each section including

    –a quiz

    –a hands-on project

    –a cooperative learning activity

    –a cross-curriculum activity

    –an extension into the reader's own life

- Post-reading Activities

- Book Report Ideas

- Research Ideas

- Culminating Activity

- Three Different Options for Unit Tests

- Bibliography of Related Reading

- Answer Key

We are confident this unit will be a valuable addition to your planning and hope that as you use our ideas, your students will increase the circle of friends they have in books!

Sample Lesson Plan

Lesson 1
- Introduce and complete some or all of the pre-reading activities found on page 5.
- Read "About the Authors" with your students (page 6).
- Introduce Section 1 vocabulary (page 8).

Lesson 2
- Read chapters 1 through 4, placing the vocabulary in context.
- Choose a vocabulary activity (page 9).
- Write a narrative story (page 11).
- Learn about interior decorating, Mr. Popper style (pages 12 and 13).
- Learn about penguins (pages 14 and 15).
- Begin reading response journals (page 16).
- Administer the Section 1 quiz (page 10).
- Introduce Section 2 vocabulary (page 8).

Lesson 3
- Read chapters 5 through 9, placing the vocabulary in context.
- Choose a vocabulary activity (page 9).
- Write a town ordinance (page 18).
- Learn to improvise (page 19).
- Find out about penguin eggs (page 20).
- Learn about buying a pet (page 21).
- Administer the Section 2 quiz (page 17).
- Introduce Section 3 vocabulary (page 8).

Lesson 4
- Read chapters 10 through 13, placing the vocabulary in context.
- Choose a vocabulary activity (page 9).
- Write cinquains (page 23).
- Create a class newspaper (page 24).
- Learn about temperature (page 25).
- Consider music appreciation (page 26).
- Administer the Section 3 quiz (page 22).
- Introduce Section 4 vocabulary (page 8).

Lesson 5
- Read chapters 14 through 17, placing the vocabulary in context.
- Choose a vocabulary activity (page 9).
- Write a critical review (page 28).
- Create a marketing campaign (page 29).
- Learn about mapping (page 30).
- Conduct an interview (page 31).
- Administer the Section 4 quiz (page 27).
- Introduce Section 5 vocabulary (page 8).

Lesson 6
- Read chapters 18 through 20, placing the vocabulary in context.
- Do a vocabulary crossword (page 33).
- Hold a debate (page 34).
- Make a balloon globe (page 35).
- Write letters home (page 36).
- Administer the Section 5 quiz (page 32).

Lesson 7
- Discuss any questions students have about the book (page 37).
- Assign book reports and research projects (pages 38 and 39).
- Begin work on the culminating activity (pages 40–42).

Lesson 8
- Administer unit tests 1, 2, and/or 3 (pages 43–45).
- Discuss the students' enjoyment of the book.
- Provide a list of related reading for your students (page 46).
- Work on the culminating activity.

Lesson 9
- Discuss the test answers and possibilities.
- Work on the culminating activity.

Lesson 10
- Present the culminating activity to the class.

Before the Book

Before you begin reading *Mr. Popper's Penguins* with your students, do some pre-reading activities to stimulate interest and to enhance future comprehension. Here are some activities that may work well in your class.

1. Predict what the story might be about by hearing the title.

2. Predict what the story might be about by looking at the cover illustration.

3. As a means of prediction, choose an illustration from each section. Have the students attempt to arrange them in the correct order to create a storyboard for the entire book.

4. Discuss what the students already know about

   - penguins
   - pets
   - painting
   - Antarctica
   - theaters/plays

5. Answer these questions:

   - Would you ever
     - leave your family?
     - write a letter to someone famous?
     - go to Antarctica?
     - take your pet on a bus?

   - Are you interested in
     - stories about animals?
     - exotic pets?
     - traveling across the United States?

6. Discuss the responsibility of caring for a pet.

7. Discuss the fiction genre and its characteristics.

About the Authors

Born Frederick Mund Atwater on December 29, 1892, in Chicago, Illinois, Richard Atwater had his name legally changed in 1913. In 1921, he married Florence, and the couple had two children, Doris and Carroll.

Throughout his life, Mr. Atwater had many occupations. He was a professor at the University of Chicago and a columnist for two newspapers, *The Evening Post* and the *Daily News of Chicago*. He also served in the army from 1918–1919. He began to write *Mr. Popper's Penguins* after attending a film with his family about Admiral Byrd's Antarctic expedition. However, it was one of his daughters who was ultimately responsible for *Mr. Popper's Penguins* being written. She objected to all the historical backgrounds included in juvenile books at the time, so Mr. Atwater decided to create a book she could enjoy.

According to his daughter, Carroll, the original manuscript contained more fantasy than the published book does now. Captain Cook actually came to life after Mr. Popper drew him on a mirror with shaving cream! Certainly, Mr. Atwater had an excellent imagination.

While still working on the manuscript, Mr. Atwater became ill and died. His wife, Florence, found his manuscript in a desk drawer. She took it to several publishing companies, but they were not interested. She decided to rewrite the beginning and the end.

Mr. Popper's Penguins was published in 1938 to great success. It immediately became a bestseller. In 1939, it won the Newbery Award. Additional awards for the book include the Young Reader's Choice Award from the Northwest Library Association in 1941 and the Lewis Carroll Shelf Award in 1958. Since its publication, the book has been translated into several languages, including Italian, Dutch, German, Spanish, Swedish, and Japanese.

Florence Hasseltine Carroll Atwater was born September 13, 1896, and she died August 23, 1979. She attended the University of Chicago where she studied French literature. For awhile, she taught high school French, English, and Latin.

Richard Atwater wrote only one additional adolescent novel: *Doris and the Trolls* (Rand McNally, 1931).

6

Mr. Popper's Penguins

by Richard and Florence Atwater

(Dell, 1938, 1978)

(Canada, Doubleday Dell Seal; UK, Bantam Doubleday Dell; AUS, Transworld Publishers)

Mr. Popper makes a living as a house painter in a small town. His life is very ordinary throughout most of the year, but during the winter, when he has no work, he spends his time reading about Antarctica and traveling around the world in his imagination. While Mr. Popper reads, Mrs. Popper worries about money.

Enthused by his readings, Mr. Popper writes a letter to Admiral Drake, an Antarctic explorer. One night, while listening to the radio, Mr. Popper hears a message from Admiral Drake. He is sending Mr. Popper a surprise from Antarctica, and the surprise turns out to be a penguin. The Popper family names the penguin Captain Cook, and they clean out a refrigerator for the little creature to live inside.

When Captain Cook becomes ill, Mr. Popper writes to a museum curator for advice. In response, the curator sends a female penguin to the Poppers. He believes that both penguins are suffering from loneliness and that they need each other's company to get better. The Poppers name their new friend Greta.

To make the penguins happy, Mr. Popper creates a winter wonderland in the family basement. Soon, just as Mrs. Popper predicts, ten eggs appear and then quickly hatch. With twelve penguins to feed, Mrs. Popper is more worried about money than ever before. To solve their problem, the family creates a trained penguin act called Mr. Popper's Performing Penguins. The act consists of three skits by the penguins, performed to different types of music. Mr. Popper finds an agent, Mr. Greenbaum, for his penguins, and together they begin to tour the United States. Mrs. Popper no longer worries about money.

One day, Mr. Popper accidentally takes his act to the wrong theater, and he is arrested for causing so much trouble. Admiral Drake bails Mr. Popper and the penguins out of jail. He then tells Mr. Popper about a new expedition to the North Pole that he will be leading. Admiral Drake would like to take the penguins with him to establish a penguin colony. However, an agent in Hollywood wants to use the penguins in movies and commercials. Mr. Popper decides to send the penguins to the North Pole with Admiral Drake. To the family's surprise, the admiral wants Mr. Popper to go along on the trip. Mr. Popper accepts, and they sail for the North Pole. Finally, Mr. Popper is able to lead an adventure he had only dreamed of before!

Vocabulary Lists

On this page are vocabulary lists that correspond to each sectional grouping of chapters. Vocabulary activity ideas can be found on page 9 of this book.

Section 1

expedition	suitable	debris	authority
pompously	bungalow	solemnly	inquisitive
calcimine	heathen	admiral	bore
erect	regret	spattered	

Section 2

rookery	spectacle	boric	astonishment
intention	stubborn	humble	dodo
ordinance	dignity	idle	determined
derby	reluctant	municipal	

Section 3

cease	portable	spar	sleek
sulk	rotogravure	refreshing	fond
curator	sympathetic	droll	
tremendous	blizzard	stupor	

Section 4

necessary	terms	unique	squawking
indulgence	exhibit	shrill	sensation
prostrate	unforeseen	rehearsal	novelty
delicate	discipline	vigorous	

Section 5

burly	furnish	lack	climate
haggard	vexed	extraordinary	fierce
apparent	familiar	breed	influence
gangplank	advantage	hoarse	

8

Vocabulary Activity Ideas

You can help your students learn and retain the vocabulary in *Mr. Popper's Penguins* by providing them with interesting vocabulary activities. Here are a few ideas to try.

❑ Challenge the class to a **vocabulary bee.** In addition to spelling each word correctly, they must also give the correct meaning. Give one point for spelling the word correctly and another for the definition.

❑ Have the students create a **class book** of crossword puzzles and word finds. They must also include the answer key.

❑ Challenge the students to rewrite a page of the story using **synonyms and antonyms** of the vocabulary words.

❑ In groups, have the students create a **picture dictionary** for one or all of the sections.

❑ Challenge students to **write an original story,** using as many of the vocabulary words as they can.

❑ Play **charades,** using the vocabulary words as clues.

❑ Challenge students to **write a fable** that explains how three words got their meaning.

❑ Use the words to play **bingo.** Have the students make their own Bingo cards and randomly write some of the words in the squares. Beans or buttons can be used as markers. Read the word definitions but not the words. Students must determine the word based on the definition only.

❑ Play **hangman** in pairs or as a whole class with the vocabulary words.

❑ Make **vocabulary journals** in which the students list words with which they are unfamiliar but do not appear on the teacher-supplied list.

❑ The book itself was translated into many different languages. **Translate the vocabulary words** and post them around the room.

❑ Play **vocabulary concentration.** The purpose of the game is to match the definition with the correct words. Divide the class into groups of approximately four. Then instruct the groups to make the cards. On one set of cards, they should write the words. On another set of cards, they should write the definitions. All cards are then shuffled and placed face down on the table. On his or her turn, each player draws two cards. If they go together, the player gets another turn. The game is played until all matches are made. A super concentration game could be played by combining vocabulary from all the sections. The game also makes a good review at the end of the book.

❑ Have the students **create a board game** that uses the vocabulary words. This can be done in cooperative groups over a period of a few days. When the boards are complete, the class should have the opportunity to play each game.

❑ Keep a **word wall** in your room. When students find a new vocabulary word in their reading, have them write the new word, its definition, and a sentence using the word on an index card or sentence strip. Staple it to a bulletin board set aside for this purpose.

There are many more ways to practice vocabulary skills. Add your own ideas! Be creative!

Quiz Time

1. On the back of this paper, write a one-paragraph summary of the section.

2. What does Mr. Popper do for a living? Why is he not working?

   _____

   _____

3. What does Mr. Popper read about? Why does he like it so much?

   _____

   _____

4. How does Mr. Popper get his penguin?

   _____

   _____

5. How does Captain Cook get his name?

   _____

   _____

6. How does Mrs. Popper react to Captain Cook?

   _____

   _____

7. How would your parents react if you brought home a new pet?

   _____

   _____

8. Why does Captain Cook sleep in the refrigerator?

   _____

   _____

9. Name someone famous to whom you would like to write. Why did you choose that person?

   _____

   _____

10. What place would you like to read about? Tell why.

    _____

    _____

Writing a Narrative Story

A narrative story describes the way in which events happen. An important aspect of a narrative is called point of view. The point of view refers to who is telling the story.

Mr. Popper's Penguins is a narrative because it describes the events caused by the arrival of Captain Cook. It is told in the third person (he, she, it, they) by a narrator, someone who is not involved in the story but is able to see what everyone is doing and thinking. A third person is someone who is not involved in the story but is able to see what everyone is doing and thinking.

Another type of point of view is called first person. In first person, a narrator tells the story from personal experience as it is happening (or happened) to him or her. In a first-person story, the narrator uses "I."

For this section, you will write a short, narrative story. Select a point of view and use it to describe Captain Cook's journey from Antarctica to Stillwater. Before you write your rough draft, it will help to brainstorm.

Point of View: _____

1. What is Captain Cook's mode of transportation?

   _____

   _____

2. How long does his journey take?

   _____

   _____

3. How does he feel on the different parts of his journey?

   _____

   _____

4. Are there any problems on the trip?

   _____

   _____

Once you have gathered your thoughts, write your story.

Interior Decorating, Mr. Popper Style

Mr. Popper unintentionally creates a decorating fad when he accidentally paints a kitchen green and yellow. Based on this principle, imagine that you and a group of friends have created an interior decorating company. Your first customer has just come to you, wanting to decorate his entire house in the same manner. The color combinations of the home are up to you. However, there are two restrictions: each room must have a different color combination, and the customer wants to see a model before you start painting.

So, where do you begin? A color wheel will help. Color the two wheels below as indicated. Cut out the wheels and assemble them together at the center dots by attaching the smaller wheel to the larger with a brass fastener. You can then turn the top wheel and view the different color combinations. You will need a total of six combinations. Write the combinations on which your company decides in the spaces provided on page 13. You will also need to determine how each of the rooms connects to the hallway.

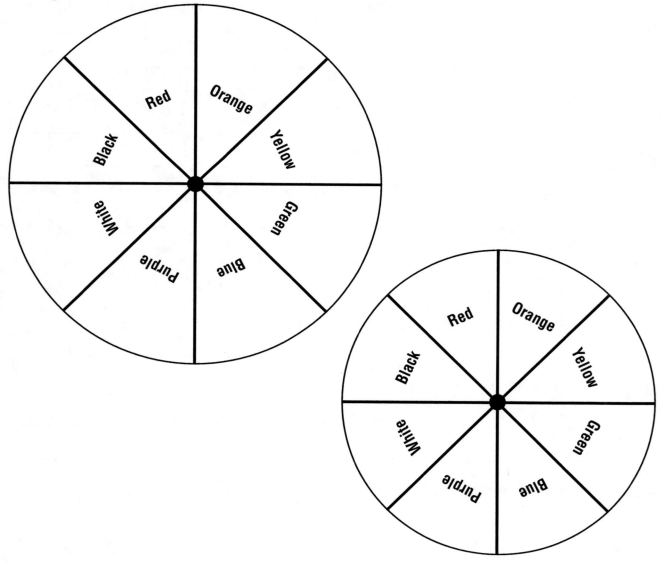

Interior Decorating, Mr. Popper Style *(cont.)*

Color Combinations:

1. Kitchen and Dining Room _____

2. Living Room _____

3. Bathroom_____

4. Bedroom 1_____

5. Bedroom 2_____

6. Hallway _____

Now, you must build your model to show your customer. Use boxes of proportionate size to construct a three-dimensional model based on a floor plan similar to the one below. Paint the walls according to your color combination choices.

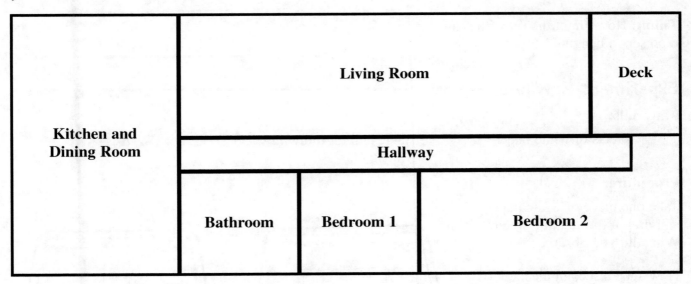

Finally, answer these questions in preparation for your presentation to your customer. Use the back of this paper.

1. How much will you charge for the job?

2. How long will it take to complete?

3. Why did you choose these color combinations?

4. Why should the customer choose your company?

Is a Penguin a Bird?

When you think of a bird, you usually think of flight. A penguin does not fly through the air, but it is still a bird. Think of the penguin as a bird that "flies" through the water.

In order to see how a penguin has adapted traditional bird characteristics to the cold Antarctic climate, you will do three experiments. After each experiment, there will be a discussion about your observations.

Experiment 1: Buoyancy

Materials:

- 2 coffee cans
- sink
- water
- sand or rocks

Procedure:

Place two coffee cans in a sink full of water. Fill one can halfway with sand or rocks. Observe what happens.

Think: How might the tin with sand represent a penguin?

Experiment 2: Wings

Materials:

- 2 sheets of white paper
- large sink or tub with water

Procedure:

Take one piece of white paper and drag it through the water. What did you observe?

Now, take a second piece of paper and fold it along its length five or six times. Drag this piece of paper through the water. What did you observe?

Think: What conclusion can you make about the wings of a penguin?

Is a Penguin a Bird? *(cont.)*

Experiment 3: Nests ——————————————————————————

Materials:

- beach balls

Procedure:

Many birds use twigs to build nests in trees. However, these materials are not available in Antarctica. How do penguins incubate their eggs? They take turns sitting on them!

Experience what it is like for penguins to incubate their eggs by using the beach balls to represent penguin eggs. Can you balance the ball on the top of your feet like a penguin does its eggs? Can you trade the "egg" with a partner? Make sure everyone gets a chance to try incubating the egg.

Record your response here:

_____

_____

_____

_____

_____

Discuss with your teacher how the penguin has adapted other traditional bird characteristics. Use encyclopedias and trade books. Then use the pattern on this page to create your own penguin rookery. In the penguin's stomach, write one fact about penguins that you find interesting. Color the penguin and cut it out. Place it somewhere on Antarctic ice.

Reading Response Journals

A great way to keep track of the students' comprehension of *Mr. Popper's Penguins* is the use of reading response journals. You can incorporate them into your daily plans or use them less often, if you prefer. You can also encourage your students to use them on their own when they read. Here are a few ideas for how to make the most of them.

❑ Create the journal as a class activity. Students can assemble the journals using both lined and unlined paper fastened with brass fasteners in a construction paper folder. Students should have time to personalize the front cover.

❑ Explain the purpose of the journal. Students should know they can record their thoughts, responses, and questions as they read each chapter or section.

❑ The journals can be used to respond to critical thinking questions that promote thought and writing. These can be given orally or written on the board for reference. Sample questions for Section 1 include the following:

   ◆ Describe a time you went someplace new. Include your feelings.

   ◆ How might the life of the Poppers change when Captain Cook arrives? What problems might they have?

❑ Ask students to use their imaginations and descriptions in the book to draw pictures of certain scenes or characters on the blank pages of their journals. Below the pictures they can write captions.

Students should know from the beginning of the project how the journals will be evaluated, if at all. There are many evaluation methods one may use. Here are a few suggestions.

❑ All entries will be read by the teacher, but no subjective grade will be given. A participation credit will be awarded to those who put forth appropriate effort.

❑ For a "grade," one can evaluate the quantity and effort put into the entries. Give students a scale similar to the following so that they are the ones to decide their grades.

   7 entries = A
   6 entries = B
   5 entries = C and so forth

❑ Have the students do a self-evaluation. On the last page of their journal, they can describe how they think the journal did or did not help them while reading the book. Do they think they put forth enough effort? What did they like best about it? and so forth.

Quiz Time

1. On the back of this paper, write a one-paragraph summary of the section.

2. What does Mr. Popper want the service man to do and why?

   _____

   _____

3. Does Mr. Popper get a license for Captain Cook? Explain.

   _____

   _____

4. List the kinds of things (at least five) that Captain Cook picks up around the house for his nest.

   _____

   _____

5. List three things that Captain Cook could pick up in your room.

   _____

   _____

6. What does Mr. Popper wear on the walk?

   _____

   _____

7. What happens on the walk Mr. Popper and Captain Cook take?

   _____

   _____

8. If you were the reporter in the book, write one question that you would ask Mr. Popper.

   _____

   _____

9. How would you react to a strange pet on a leash?

   _____

   _____

10. Suppose your parents told you to get dirty. How would you like to do it?

   _____

   _____

Town Ordinance

Hear ye! Hear ye! Rules are everywhere in society. Can you list three rules from your home, school, or community that affect you?

1. _____
   _____

2. _____
   _____

3. _____
   _____

Mr. Popper is affected by rules, too! However, he is not always sure what the rules concerning penguins are. Help him by making a class book of *Stillwater Penguin Ordinances*. Everyone in the class must write an ordinance for a different place. Suggested places include restaurants, movie theaters, shopping malls, and parks. Write your ordinance in outline form like the one below.

Stillwater Penguin Ordinance #_____

    I. The place

    II. What the penguin can do

        A.

        B.

    III. What the penguin can not do

        A.

        B.

    IV. What happens if the penguin breaks the rules

    V. When the law is in effect

Here are some things to consider before you begin writing.

1. For what place are you writing your law?

2. How will the other people feel about the penguin?

3. What may the penguin do? not do?

4. Does Mr. Popper have to do anything special to the penguin?

5. Are there time limits involved?

Improvisation as Drama

Improvisational skits in the classroom allow students to relieve stress and excess energy. They can also add a bit of humor to brighten a stressful or rainy day.

The only preparation needed for this activity is a discussion of emotions and related body language. With your class, list different emotions on the board. Once this is done, ask for volunteers to demonstrate how each emotion "looks."

The next step is to explain improvisation as an acting technique. Then divide the class into small groups. Each group will go to the "stage." Give each group a situation from chapter sections 1 or 2 to act out. Their only directions will be to perform the skit, showing the different emotions. You may want to allow a short period of time to let the students assign parts and gather props.

This activity is particularly good because it will assess the students' overall comprehension. Remember, it is improvisation! There is not a great deal of preparation that goes into an improvisational performance.

Here are some suggested scenes to perform from chapter sections 1 and 2:

- **Mr. Popper and Captain Cook meet a neighbor on their walk.**

- **Captain Cook is in the barber shop.**

- **The service man comes to the house.**

- **Janie and Bill meet Captain Cook for the first time.**

- **The policeman talks to Mr. Popper.**

After each scene is performed, ask students in the audience to identify which emotions were portrayed and how. For a little fun, the teacher may consider handing out a "Quick Thinking" award to all who participated.

"Eggs"traordinary!

Like all birds, penguins lay eggs in order to reproduce. Everyone knows that eggs have a shell on the outside to protect the developing chick, but do you know what is on the inside to help the baby bird?

A. Read the description below telling about the parts of an egg. Then write the egg parts on the correct lines of the diagram.

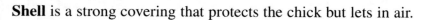

Albumen, usually the white part, creates a protective layer around the chick.

Chalaza is a rope-like structure that acts as an anchor.

Membrane is two skin-like layers that form an **air pocket** near the shell.

Shell is a strong covering that protects the chick but lets in air.

Yolk serves as a food source for the developing chick.

B. Now that the parts are labeled, look at an egg cracked open into a dish. Can you identify all the parts?

C. Try these "eggs"tension experiments with everyday household items. Amaze your parents with the impossible!

1. Will an egg float?

Materials: 2 glasses of water, 1 measuring teaspoon, 1 raw egg, salt

Procedure: Gently place the egg in each glass of water. Watch what happens. Next, add a teaspoon (5 mL) of salt to one glass and stir completely. Add more salt, a teaspoon (5 mL) at a time, until the egg floats. How many teaspoons (mL) did it take?

2. Can you see through an eggshell?

Materials: 1 raw egg, vinegar, bowl

Procedure: Soak a raw egg in vinegar overnight. There should be enough vinegar to cover the egg completely. The vinegar will take the calcium out of the eggshell while it soaks. Take the egg out of the bowl and rinse it off. What do you notice? Record your observations below.

_____

_____

_____

_____

Which One Would You Buy?

Mr. Popper's pet is sent to him as a surprise. Most families, however, spend a great deal of time picking out the perfect pet. Suppose your family was thinking about getting a new pet. You would need to think carefully about everything involved before purchasing your new friend.

Next to each animal on this page is a set of two questions. Answer the questions, using your prior knowledge, books about the animals, and encyclopedias.

1. How much does a dog eat each day?

   _____

2. Can a dog be dangerous to anyone? How?

   _____

1. What medical bills might a cat incur?

   _____

2. Will a cat cause any damage to your home?

   _____

1. Are there any veterinarian bills involved with a mouse?

   _____

2. How much does mouse food cost?

   _____

1. Is there any cleaning involved with a snake?

   _____

2. What can you feed a snake?

   _____

1. Can fish get sick?

   _____

2. How expensive are fish and aquariums?

   _____

Quiz Time

1. On the back of this paper, write a one-paragraph summary of the section.

2. How do the Poppers know that something is wrong with Captain Cook?

   _____

   _____

3. Does Captain Cook get better? Explain what happens.

   _____

   _____

4. If you were sick, what would you do to get better?

   _____

   _____

5. What does Mrs. Popper predict? Is she right? Explain.

   _____

   _____

6. If you could rename all the penguin babies, what would you name them?

   _____

   _____

   _____

7. Describe what Mr. Popper does to the basement.

   _____

   _____

8. How are the Poppers going to solve their money problems? Be specific.

   _____

   _____

   _____

9. What is another way the Poppers could get money?

   _____

   _____

10. What is on Mr. Popper's mind?

   _____

Writing Cinquains

Not all poems must rhyme. One kind of poem that does not rhyme is a cinquain. These five-lined poems are written according to the number of syllables in each line. While reading the cinquain below, clap along to count the syllables in each line. Count the number of syllables in each line. Can you find the pattern?

Penguins

funny, playful

swimming, waddling, flapping

milling about their rookery

Penguins

You should have found that the syllable pattern is 2, 4, 6, 8, and 2. However, a cinquain also has a second pattern to follow. Each of the five lines has a specific purpose.

> Line 1 – One word that names the subject
>
> Line 2 – Two adjectives that describe the subject
>
> Line 3 – Three verbs that express what the subject does
>
> Line 4 – Four-word phrase about the subject
>
> Line 5 – A synonym for the subject or the subject repeated

In the space below, write your own cinquain about something or someone in *Mr. Popper's Penguins*. Be sure to count your syllables and to follow the cinquain pattern.

_____

_____

_____

_____

_____

So You're Making a Newspaper

A newspaper is not easy to produce. It takes time and cooperation from the entire staff. To make a class newspaper, you will have to work cooperatively to get the job done, and everyone will need to pitch in to get it done well.

You are going to create a class newspaper about *Mr. Popper's Penguins.* Here are some helpful tips to get you started.

1. Decide what parts you want your newspaper to have. You must have a story about Mr. Popper, weather, sports, and entertainment. However you can add anything else you want, as well.

2. Remember that a news story must include who, what, when, where, why, and how in order to get all the information to the reader.

3. Decide on a name for your paper.

4. Decide on a format for your paper. Consider these questions:
   • Where are you going to put everything?
   • How many pages are you going to have?
   • How will you create the final copy?
   • Will you have illustrations?

5. Newspapers should be free of spelling and punctuation errors, so be very careful when you make your final copy.

6. Decide who is going to write which parts. Remember, you are a team.

Newspaper Name _____

Staff Members	Assignment(s)

Note: If you have any questions, ask the editor in chief (teacher).

What's It Like Outside?

Mr. Popper leaves the windows open during the winter so the penguins will be more comfortable. However, by doing so, the Popper family is cold and must wear their coats inside the house.

Penguins live in Antarctica where it is cold all year long. They have a layer of fat to keep their bodies warm. Humans also have fat to insulate their bodies, but our seasons change and so does the temperature. In the space below, describe what the weather is probably like at the given temperature.

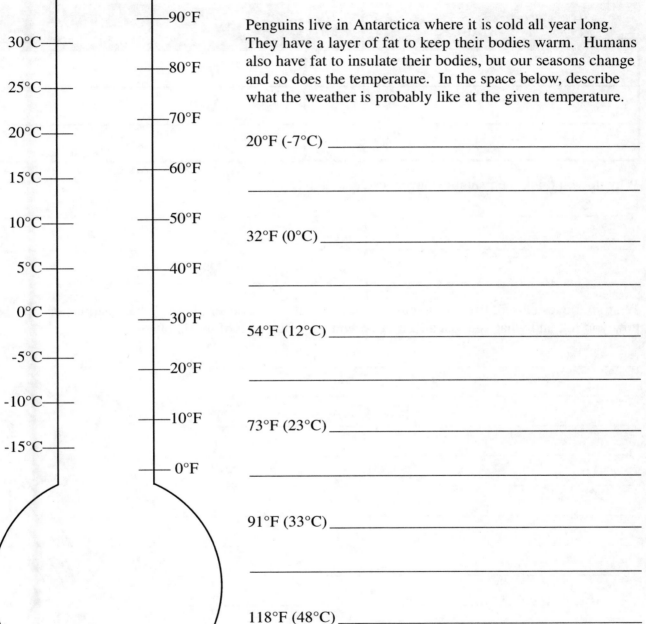

20°F (-7°C) _____

_____

32°F (0°C) _____

_____

54°F (12°C) _____

_____

73°F (23°C) _____

_____

91°F (33°C) _____

_____

118°F (48°C) _____

_____

Color the thermometer with red to indicate the temperature outside today. On the back, describe the weather.

Music Appreciation

Different kinds of music make the penguins act in certain ways. List their reactions to three kinds of music.

Music	Reaction
1.	
2.	
3.	

Why do you think the penguins have these reactions?

_____

_____

_____

With your eyes closed, listen to a music selection that your teacher plays. When the music stops, write how you felt and what you visualized. Can you name the type of music played?

_____

_____

_____

_____

_____

_____

_____

_____

On the back, describe what kind of act Popper's Performing Penguins might do to the music selection you just heard.

Quiz Time

1. On the back of this paper, write a one-paragraph summary of the section.

2. What happens on the bus?

   _____

   _____

3. How does Mrs. Popper play the piano? Why?

   _____

   _____

4. How does Columbus win the sparring match? Is it fair?

   _____

   _____

5. How much is Mr. Greenbaum going to pay the Poppers? What do they do with the first check?

   _____

   _____

6. How would you spend the money?

   _____

   _____

   _____

7. What kind of ice cream do the penguins get?

   _____

8. Why are the Poppers late for the train?

   _____

   _____

9. Why do you think the penguins have to ride in the baggage car of the train?

   _____

   _____

10. Describe how the penguins interfere in one other act.

   _____

   _____

   _____

You Be the Critic

Teacher Note: Collect a variety of reviews (movies, books, etc.) from the newspaper and bring them to into class. Then distribute the assignment below.

- -

Before many people see a play, movie, or opera, they read a review in the newspaper to find out if a critic thought it was good. A critic is someone who reviews these events and writes about the good and bad parts for the newspaper or television. Read the reviews your teacher brought into class. Discuss with your classmates whether or not the critic thought the object of the review was any good. How can you tell?

Now, use your imagination to pretend you are a newspaper critic. Your assignment is to review *Popper's Performing Penguins*.

Here are some things to consider:

1. What did you like about the performance?
2. What didn't you like about the performance?
3. How did you feel during the performance?
4. What suggestions do you have?

Brainstorm your ideas here. Write your review on the back.

_____

_____

_____

_____

_____

_____

_____

_____

_____

_____

When your review is ready, it will be collected with everyone else's review to make a class anthology. Discuss your findings and the consensus of the class.

Popper's Penguins: Take 1

Welcome to Hollywood! You are in charge of making a commercial for a product, using Popper's Performing Penguins as your "spokes" penguins. You have one week to prepare your commercial. If done right, you could make millions. Good luck!

Helpful tips to get you started:

1. Decide on a product.

2. Come up with a slogan or jingle.

3. Decide on how you are going to present your commercial. You may act it out or draw it on storyboards. If you act it out, be sure to have props ready. **Note:** Everyone in the group must have a part in the presentation or take part in creating and presenting the storyboards.

4. You are trying to sell a product, so remember to look your audience in the eye when you give your presentation.

5. If you have any questions, ask the producer (teacher).

Group Members:

1. _____

2. _____

3. _____

4. _____

5. _____

Product:_____

Slogan or Jingle:_____

_____

_____

_____

_____

Mapping It Out

The Poppers are on the road for ten weeks. In that time, they go to nine different cities. List the cities on the lines below and mark each one with a small dot on the map. Then connect the dots.

_____

_____

Use the scale to figure out the miles (kilometers) traveled from one city to the other as asked below. Be sure to include the miles (kilometers) traveled to get through all the cities between the two given places.

1. Seattle to Milwaukee _____

2. Chicago to Detroit _____

3. Philadelphia to Boston _____

4. Minneapolis to Cleveland _____

5. Seattle to Boston _____

Let's Talk

Mr. Popper has agreed to do an interview with your class this week. In order to do a good interview, you must prepare your questions ahead of time. In the spaces below, write five questions that you would like to ask Mr. Popper about himself, his family, the penguins, or his trip to the North Pole.

1. _____

   _____

   _____

2. _____

   _____

3. _____

   _____

4. _____

   _____

5. _____

   _____

On the day of the interview, everyone will be able to ask one question. Star the question you would most like to ask.

On the back, discuss your feelings and thoughts about the entire interview.

- -

Teacher Note: A staff member, parent volunteer, or friend must play the role of Mr. Popper. This person needs to be familiar with the events of the book and Mr. Popper's character overall.

Quiz Time

1. On the back of this paper, write a one-paragraph summary of the section.

2. What mistake does Mr. Popper make?

   _____

   _____

3. What happens as a result of his mistake?

   _____

   _____

4. Name one mistake you have made and tell what happened.

   _____

   _____

5. What happens to the penguins while they are in jail?

   _____

   _____

6. Who pays Mr. Popper's bail?

   _____

   _____

7. What are Mr. Popper's choices for the penguins?

   _____

   _____

8. Why is Mrs. Popper getting $25,000?

   _____

   _____

9. Does Mr. Popper make a wise decision? Why or why not?

   _____

   _____

10. Name three things Mr. Popper should take on the trip with him. Tell why they are needed.

   _____

   _____

   _____

Vocabulary Review Crossword

Across
4. weather conditions of a region
5. to produce offspring
7. better position or chance
10. obvious
11. to supply
12. worn appearance
13. be without something

Down
1. power to change something
2. low and husky in sound
3. mean or violent
5. strong
6. common
8. irritated
9. used as a ramp on a ship

Debate

We make many decisions everyday: what to wear, buy, do, and so forth. Before we make any decisions, however, we think about the advantages and disadvantages of our decisions. Some decisions are more complicated than others and require more thought.

Mr. Popper has a very hard decision to make at the end of the book. What decision does he make?

_____

_____

Which option do you think he should have chosen?

_____

_____

You will be put in a group with those who made the same choice as you. As a team, you will have a debate with the other team to determine which decision is better. In order for the debate to work, both sides have to prepare arguments for their choice. Use the back of this paper to list all the advantages and disadvantages of your team's decision. Your teacher will monitor the debate and serve as the judge.

After the debate, list at least three arguments the opposite team made in defense of their decision.

1. _____

_____

2. _____

_____

3. _____

_____

Now that you have heard both sides, how do you feel about the subject?

_____

_____

_____

Make a Balloon Globe

You will have the world in your hands when you finish this activity! Here is what you will need:

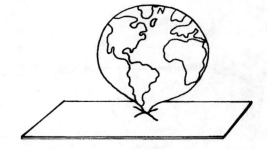

- 9" (22.5 cm) blue balloon
- 4" (10 cm) square piece of poster board
- black permanent marker
- green permanent markert
- globe (as a reference)

Directions:

1. Blow up the balloon and tie the end. Be careful not to overfill the balloon. You want to keep a round shape. The knot will represent the South Pole.

2. Use the marker to mark the North Pole.

3. Draw all seven continents on the balloon. Be careful not to press too hard or the balloon may pop.

4. Cut a small X in the middle of the poster board square. Insert the knot of the balloon through the opening so that the balloon will stand up straight.

5. Fill in the continents with green marker.

6. When the balloon is dry, draw the prime meridian and equator with the black marker.

7. Answer these questions:

   a. What continents does the equator pass through?

   _____

   _____

   b. What continents does the prime meridian pass through?

   _____

   _____

   c. Where do the prime meridian and equator intersect?

   _____

   _____

   d. Use the marker to indicate your city on the globe. How far east is it from the prime meridian?

   _____

   How far north is it from the equator? _____

Letters Home

For this activity, you must pretend that you are a crew member on Admiral Drake's expedition to the North Pole. Before you left, your family asked you to write a letter that tells them about your trip.

*Date*_____

Dear _____,

_____

_____

_____

_____

_____

_____

_____

_____

_____

_____

_____

Love,

_____

Before you begin writing, you may want to brainstorm answers to some of the following questions and include the information in your letter: What events have occurred? How do you feel? Are there any problems? What does the North Pole look like? When you are ready, use the friendly letter format above to write your letter.

Any Questions?

When you finished reading *Mr. Popper's Penguins*, did you have some questions that were left unanswered? Write some of your questions here.

_____

_____

_____

_____

_____

_____

_____

_____

Work in groups or by yourself to prepare possible answers for some or all of the questions you have asked above and those written below. When you have finished your predictions, share your ideas with the class.

- Does Mr. Popper return home? How? When? How has Stillwater changed since he left?

- Is the expedition to establish a penguin colony at the North Pole successful? Why or why not?

- How does Mrs. Popper spend the $25,000?

- What will Mr. Popper read about now? Why?

- To whom will Mr. Popper write next? What will he write?

- How are Janie and Bill received at school after being away for so long?

- What happens to the penguin family?

- On what expedition will Admiral Drake go next? Give details.

- What does Mrs. Popper do while Mr. Popper is away?

- Does the family get another pet? If so, what kind? Why do they choose this type of pet?

Book Report Ideas

There are many ways to share a book you have just finished reading. Choose one activity from the list below or create one of your own to share *Mr. Popper's Penguins* with the school and your family.

- **Performance**

  With a partner, act out your favorite scene from the book for another class. Be sure to arrange a time with the other teacher. Consider whether or not you will read cards, memorize, or improvise. You may want to consider costumes.

- **Book Review**

  Write a critical review of the book for the school newspaper. Be sure to include your responses to questions such as these: Would you recommend it? Why or why not? What do you like most about it?

- **Book Jacket**

  Design a new cover for the book. Remember to include the author's name, the title, and a short summary on the back. Do not forget the spine of the book. Get supplies from your teacher.

- **Diorama**

  Make a three-dimensional picture of your favorite scene in a small box and display it in the library with a short summary of the book. Be sure to ask your librarian if there is a special spot in which your project can be displayed.

- **Interview**

  With a partner, pretend that you will be interviewing a character from the book on a television show. One person should be the host, and the other should be the character. You can conduct the interview live for the class or tape it and show it at a pre-arranged time.

  Write a radio or television commercial advertising the book. Record it on tape or perform it live at a pre-arranged time for your class or another class. You may want to consider the use of props, costumes, and samples of the product.

- **Penguin Performance**

  In a group of three or four, create a fourth act for the penguins to perform on their tour. Perform it for your class. You must pick the music and decide how the penguins would react to it. Explain this to the class after your performance.

- **Sequel**

  Write an introduction for the sequel to the book. It should be at least five typed pages long. You might consider these topics: Mr. Popper's experience at the North Pole; the boat ride; how the penguins liked the north; what the rest of the Popper family did in Stillwater while Mr. Popper was away; what happened when Mr. Popper returned.

Research Ideas

What are three things from *Mr. Popper's Penguins* about which you would like to learn more?

1. _____

2. _____

3. _____

Decide with your teacher whether you will do an individual or group project. Then decide on a topic. Use a suggestion from the list below or use one of your own. (Use the space below to write your topic ideas.) Share your research with your class in any appropriate form that you have discussed with your teacher.

- **Antarctica**
    - Exploration
    - Science at the South Pole
    - Animal Life
    - Ice Formation

- **Explorers**
    - Admiral Byrd
    - Marco Polo
    - Hernan Cortes
    - Lewis and Clark
    - Robert Scott
    - Matthew Henson
    - Leif the Lucky
    - Ferdinand Magellan
    - Henry Hudson

- **Circuses** *(Animal Acts)*
    - History
    - Ringling Brothers Circus

- **Climates of the World**
    - Differences
    - Animal Adaptation

- **Theaters**
    - History
    - Famous Theaters
    - A Famous Play or Musical
    - Role of Agents

- **Painting**
    - Types of Paint
    - Techniques Used
    - Famous Artists or Paintings

Topics

Create Your Own Animal Act

The Poppers have a successful penguin act because they plan their act with great care and spend much time practicing. Eventually, it pays off and they make $5,000 a week.

In this culminating activity, you will create your own animal act. Each step is described below and on pages 41 and 42.

A. Choose an animal species to use in your act. Use the diagram below to brainstorm ideas.

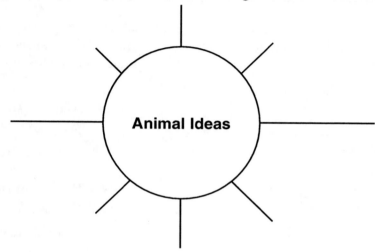

B. Choose one animal from above and explain why you are going to use it for your act.

_____

_____

_____

_____

_____

C. Answer these questions:

• How many of these animals will you use?_____

• What and how much do these animal eat? _____

• Where will you keep them? _____

Create Your Own Animal Act *(cont.)*

D. Choose the music you will use in your act. Circle three types of music from the list below.

country	jazz	classical	march
waltz	oldies	rock	opera
rap	children's	blues	alternative

E. For each of your three selections above, list a song title if you have one in mind. If not, simply write down the type of music. Then describe the act you could develop, using that song or type of music. Remember, the actions must resemble natural movements and behaviors of your animal species.

1. _____

_____

_____

_____

2. _____

_____

_____

_____

3. _____

_____

_____

_____

F. What about practice? In the space below, describe when, where, and how long you will rehearse.

_____

_____

_____

_____

Create Your Own Animal Act *(cont.)*

G. The next step is to choose cities in which to tour. Your agent wants you to tour in ten cities on the continent to which your animal is native. List the continent and the cities in order on the following lines.

Continent: _____

   1. _____

   2. _____

   3. _____

   4. _____

   5. _____

   6. _____

   7. _____

   8. _____

   9. _____

 10. _____

H. How many weeks will it take you to complete the tour? _____

I. Now, you need a catchy name for your animal act. The Poppers used an alliteration: Popper's Performing Penguins. Brainstorm an idea and write it in the box below.

┌───┐
│   │
│   │
│   │
└───┘

Why is this a catchy name?_____

_____

J. Now you need to think about money.

   1. How much will you charge for tickets? _____

   2. How much is your agent going to pay you per week? _____

   3. When the tour is over, how much will you have made?_____

   4. What expenses will you have along the way? _____

   5. What will you do with your profits?_____

Unit Test

Matching: Match the name of each character with his or her description.

_____ 1. Admiral Drake   A. a painter in Stillwater

_____ 2. Captain Cook   B. two penguins

_____ 3. Janie and Bill   C. penguin who lives in the refrigerator

_____ 4. Mr. Popper   D. explorer of the Antarctic

_____ 5. Mr. Greenbaum   E. agent with a contract

_____ 6. Scott and Jenny   F. Mr. Popper's children

True or False: Write true or false next to each statement.

_____ 1. Mr. Popper creates an act based on the penguins' reactions to music and because he needs money.

_____ 2. Popper's Performing Penguins tour Europe.

_____ 3. The story is told from Captain Cook's point of view.

_____ 4. Because the penguins are popular, they are used in a commercial for dog food.

_____ 5. Mrs. Popper plays the piano during the penguins' act.

_____ 6. There are three parts in the penguins' act.

Short Answer: Provide a short answer for each question.

1. How does Mr. Popper get Captain Cook? _____

_____

2. Why does Greta arrive? _____

_____

3. How does Mr. Popper make the penguins feel at home? _____

_____

4. Why do the penguins get off the bus? _____

_____

5. Why does Mr. Popper leave his family? _____

_____

Essay: Answer each of these questions in detail on the back of this paper. Use additional paper if you need more room.

1. Is a penguin a good pet? Why or why not?
2. How would the end of the story change if Mr. Popper did not go to the North Pole?
3. Would you have gone with the Admiral? Explain why or why not.

Response

Explain the meaning of each of these quotations from the story.

Chapter 1:   *"But what worries me is the money. I have saved a little, and I daresay we can get along as we have other winters."*

Chapter 3:   *"Perhaps," thought Mr. Popper, "all that white tiling reminds him of the ice and snow at the South Pole. Poor thing, maybe he's thirsty."*

Chapter 5:   *"I suppose now you want me to take the door off its hinges to let in a little more air."*

Chapter 8:   *"Take your South Pole goose away from me at once."*

Chapter 10:   *"I will leave you some pills. Give him one every hour. Then you can try feeding him on sherbet and wrapping him in ice packs. But I cannot give you any encouragement because I am afraid it is a hopeless case."*

Chapter 13:   *"I have a better idea. We will keep the penguins. Mamma, you have heard of trained seals, acting in theaters?"*

Chapter 14:   *"Well, if I hear any complaints, off they go at the next corner."*

Chapter 15:   *"The other penguins all like Columbus to win, and so they all say 'Gook!' at the end. That always makes Nelson look away, so Columbus can sock him good."*

Chapter 16:   *"And you must remember my love, . . . that travel is very broadening."*

Chapter 18:   *"Bill, you run out of the theater and call the police to come and try to save some of our penguins."*

Chapter 19:   *"You're free, Mr. Popper. There's a friend of yours here."*

Chapter 20:   *"I want you to know how much I appreciate your offer of putting my birds in the movies. But I am afraid I have to refuse."*

Conversations

Work in size-appropriate groups to write and perform the conversations that might have occurred in each of the following situations.

- Janie and Bill are home when Captain Cook arrives. *(2 people)*
- Mrs. Popper does not let Mr. Popper keep Captain Cook. *(2 people)*
- Admiral Drake delivers the penguin in person. *(4 people)*
- The repairman wants to buy Captain Cook. *(3 people)*
- The family discusses what to do when Greta and Captain Cook do not get along. *(6 people)*
- Neighbors confront Mr. Popper about the penguins. *(5 people)*
- Someone wants to buy a penguin egg. *(3 people)*
- The penguins discuss their feelings about the Poppers. *(12 people)*
- Friends of Bill and Janie want to see the penguins. *(5 people)*
- A bill collector comes to collect overdue payments. *(3 people)*
- A penguin gets lost in the city. *(5 or 6 people)*
- During the act, a penguin falls and gets hurt. *(7 people)*
- Mr. and Mrs. Popper discuss getting a tutor for the children. *(2 people)*
- Bill and Janie are upset about Mr. Popper leaving. *(3 people)*
- Mr. Popper does not go with the penguins and has to say goodbye to each one. *(13 people)*
- Admiral Drake asks the entire family to go on the trip. *(5 people)*

Additional idea: Perform one of your own conversations using the characters from *Mr. Popper's Penguins.* Write your conversation idea here.

_____

_____

_____

_____

_____

Bibliography of Related Reading

Asimov, Isaac. ***How Did We Find Out About Antarctica?*** (Walker, 1979)

Billings, Henry. ***Antarctica.*** (Children's Press, 1994)

Blumberg, Rhoda. ***The Incredible Journey of Lewis and Clark.*** (Lothrop, Lee and Shepard, 1987)

Carris, Joan Davenport and Dora Leder. ***Just a Little Ham.*** (Little Brown and Company, 1989)

Dewey, Jennifer Owings. ***Birds of Antarctica: The Adelie Penguin.*** (Little Brown and Co., 1989)

Gondosch, Linda. ***Brutus, the Wonder Poodle.*** (Random House, 1990)

Hargrove, Jim. ***Ferdinand Magellan.*** (Children's Press, 1990)

Keating, Bern. ***Famous American Explorers.*** (Rand McNally, 1972)

Kline, Suzy. ***Herbie Jones and Hamburger Head.*** (Putnam, 1989)

Linley, Mike. ***The Penguin, the Fastest Flightless Birds.*** (Garrett Education, 1992)

Lye, Keith. ***Take a Trip to Antarctica.*** (F. Watts, 1984)

May, John. ***The Greenpeace Book of Antarctica: A New View of the Seventh Continent.*** (Doubleday, 1989)

Ross, Stewart. ***Columbus and the Age of Exploration.*** (Bookwright Press, 1985)

Sainsing, David. ***The World of Penguins.*** (G. Stevens, 1988)

Schlein, Miriam. ***Antarctica: The Great White Continent.*** (Hastings House, 1980)

Seabrooke, Brenda. ***The Dragon That Ate Summer.*** (Scholastic, 1982)

Singer, Marilyn. ***Tarantula on the Brain.*** (Harper & Row, 1982)

Stein, R. Conrad and Richard Wahl. ***The Story of Marquette and Joliet.*** (Children's Press 1981)

Stolz, Mary. ***King Emmett the Second.*** (Greenwillow Books, 1991)

Swan, Robert. ***Destination, Antarctica.*** (Scholastic, 1988)

Switzer, Merebeth. ***Penguins.*** (Grolier, 1990)

Wepman, Dennis. ***Hernan Cortes.*** (Chelsea House, 1986)

Video

Exploring Antarctica (Questar Video, 1991)

Answer Key

Page 10

1. Accept appropriate responses.
2. Mr. Popper is a painter. He is not working because it is winter.
3. He reads about Antarctica because he wants to go there.
4. Admiral Drake sends Captain Cook to Mr. Popper as a surprise.
5. He gets his name because the sound he makes (*Gook*) resembles Cook, the last name of the famous explorer, Captain Cook.
6. Mrs. Popper is surprised and scared.
7. Accept appropriate responses.
8. He sleeps in the refrigerator because it is cold.
9. Accept appropriate responses.
10. Accept appropriate responses.

Page 17

1. Accept appropriate responses.
2. He wants the service man to drill air holes in the door and put a handle on the inside.
3. No, he does not get a license. No one understands what he is talking about.
4. Any of the following are acceptable answers: chess piece, thread, puzzle pieces, spoon, matches, radish, pennies, nickel, golf ball, card, ash tray, hairpins, olive, dominoes, sock, buttons, marbles, checkers, key, eraser, tinfoil, lemon, doll head, pipe, cork, screws, belt buckle, beads, blocks, bone, harmonica, lollipop, notebook.
5. Accept appropriate responses.
6. Mr. Popper wears a tuxedo.
7. They upset Mrs. Callahan and cause trouble in the barbershop. They are interviewed by a reporter.
8. Accept appropriate responses.
9. Accept appropriate responses.
10. Accept appropriate responses.

Page 20

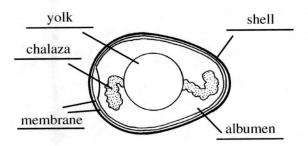

Page 22

1. Accept appropriate responses.
2. Captain Cook will not play with anyone or eat any food. He sits around all day. He has a fever.
3. Captain Cook gets better when Greta arrives. He is not lonely anymore.
4. Accept appropriate responses.
5. Mrs. Popper predicts there will be eggs. She is right because Greta lays 10 eggs.
6. Accept appropriate responses.
7. Mr. Popper installs a freezing plant in the basement, takes out the furnace, makes an ice castle, and makes a swimming/diving pool.
8. The Poppers are going to create an act and tour the country.
9. Accept appropriate answers.
10. He is thinking about what will happen when spring comes.

Page 25

Accept all appropriate answers.

Page 27

1. Accept appropriate responses.
2. Mr. Popper opens all the windows, and everyone gets cold. The driver kicks them off.
3. She plays with gloves on because it is cold in the basement.
4. Columbus wins the sparring match because the other penguins distract Nelson. When Nelson looks away, Columbus is able to knock him down.
5. He is going to pay them $5,000 a week. They pay all their bills with the first check.
6. Accept appropriate responses.
7. A flavor is not named in the book.
8. They are late because there is an accident with the taxis.
9. Accept appropriate responses.
10. Accept appropriate responses.

Answer Key

Page 30

They travel to Seattle, Milwaukee, Minneapolis, Chicago, Detroit, Cleveland, Philadelphia, Boston and New York.

Distances should be in the neighborhood of the following:

1. 1,970 miles/3177 kilometers
2. 284 miles/458 kilometers
3. 304 miles/490 kilometers
4. 879 miles/1417 kilometers
5. 3,251 miles/5243 kilometers

Page 32

1. Accept appropriate responses.
2. He goes to the wrong theater.
3. The seals and the penguins get locked in a room. People think they will hurt each other.
4. Accept appropriate responses.
5. The penguins are bored and are not getting any exercise.
6. Admiral Drake pays Mr. Popper's bail.
7. He must choose between making films and sending the penguins to the North Pole.
8. She gets $25,000 because the director makes a short film about the penguins before they leave for the North Pole.
9. Accept appropriate responses.
10. Accept appropriate answers.

Page 33

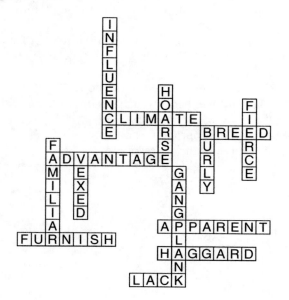

Page 43

Matching

1. d
2. c
3. f
4. a
5. e
6. b

True or False

1. True
2. False
3. False
4. False
5. True
6. True

Short Answer

1. Captain Cook is sent to Mr. Popper by Admiral Drake.
2. Greta arrives because the curator of the museum thinks both penguins are lonely.
3. He remodels the basement.
4. They are kicked off the bus.
5. Admiral Drake wants him to go to the North Pole.

Essay

1. Accept appropriate responses. Answers should reflect on the problems the Poppers have with the penguins.
2. Accept appropriate responses.
3. Accept appropriate responses.

Page 44

Accept all reasonable and well supported answers.

Page 45

After the performances, discuss whether or not the skits maintained the same characterizations presented in the book.